Louis Heylen

**The Progress of the Age and the Danger of the Age**

Louis Heylen

**The Progress of the Age and the Danger of the Age**

ISBN/EAN: 9783337371883

Printed in Europe, USA, Canada, Australia, Japan

Cover: Foto ©Suzi / pixelio.de

More available books at **www.hansebooks.com**

# THE PROGRESS OF THE AGE,

### AND THE

## DANGER OF THE AGE:

## TWO LECTURES

DELIVERED BEFORE THE ST. XAVIER CONFERENCE OF
THE ST. VINCENT DE PAUL BROTHERHOOD IN
THE HALL OF ST. LOUIS UNIVERSITY.

BY THE

## REV. LOUIS HEYLEN, S.J.

CINCINNATI:
JOHN P. WALSH, 170 SYCAMORE STREET.
1865.

# PREFACE.

The present literary compositions form part of a course of lectures delivered during the winter of 1862-63, by some of the Professors of the St. Louis University. The publication of these two lectures has been thought particularly appropriate at this time, both on account of the interesting nature of the subject and the ability with which it is treated, and as a slight tribute to the memory of the author, since deceased.

The Rev. Louis Heylen, was born at Heyst-op-den-berg, near Antwerp, Belgium, in the year 1828. He performed his first studies in the college of Mechlin, where he was distinguished for brilliant talents, and that solid piety which characterized his after-life. The account of his entry into the religious state, and of his labors in this country, we extract from a brief notice published in the *Freeman's Journal*, shortly after his death. "Animated with the desire of consecrating himself to God in the religious state, he decided upon joining the American mission, with which he had become acquainted through the writings of the venerable Father De Smet. Accordingly, at the close of his studies, crowned with the honors of his class, he renounced every prospect of eminence and emolument which his great abilities seemed to promise him, and entered the Jesuit Novitiate of Tronchiennes, Belgium. After a few months spent in that holy solitude, he was instructed to cross to the United States, along with several other young men devoted to the Missionary vocation, and arrived at St. Louis in 1848. At the close of his probation, he was admitted to the religious vows, and, having finished his philosophical studies with applause, was employed for several years in Cincinnati and elsewhere, in the various duties of a college. He was then sent to St. John's, Fordham, to go through his course of Theology, where he fully sustained his reputation for ability. On his return to the West, he passed a brilliant examination in the whole of Philosophy and Theology, and was promoted to the priesthood in 1859. From that day to his death, he was employed in many useful offices—chiefly as Professor of Philosophy in St. Xavier College, Cincinnati, where he formed a number of pupils, who will long remember his services to them. He was likewise assiduous in the confessional and pulpit. His style of oratory was earnest and vivacious, and distinguished for originality and abundance. Those who were best acquainted with his intellectual habits, regarded Father Heylen as a man of genius, remarkable for the facility with which he mastered the most profound subjects, and the clearness with which he imparted his information to others. He had, moreover, thoroughly studied the English language, and was intimately conversant with its literature. The last year of his life was spent at the St. Louis University, where he filled the chair of Poetry, with great credit to himself and advantage to his pupils. He was engaged in preparing them for their annual examination, when he was arrested in his labor by a violent malady which carried him off, after five days of suffering." His death occurred about four months after the delivery of these lectures; and it is to be hoped that, besides the good which they are otherwise calculated to effect, they will long serve as a means of keeping fresh in the minds of all who knew him, an affectionate remembrance of the talented author.

# THE AGE OF PROGRESS.

Society, like individuals, is, in all ages, distinguished by some predominant, or, at least, widely prevalent spirit; some idea, the theme of every tongue; some master passion, deeply agitating the nations; some all-absorbing or favorite impulse, governing the energies of the civilized world. It varies at different epochs, as it varies in different individuals, and constitutes the peculiar character of an age. It is the main source of the ever shifting current of events. It forms, according as it is a spirit of good or a spirit of evil, the principle of the world's greatness or degradation, the main cause of the rise and fall of empires. It explains, as far as it is given to man to understand them, the dealings of Providence with the human race. It lies at the foundation of the philosophy of history. It is so essential to a correct understanding of our age, that I deem it necessary to illustrate it by casting a rapid glance at the great epochs of history.

The earliest ages, distinguished for a while by a mighty struggle between the virtues of the race of Seth, and the vices of the children of Cain, become gradually marked by a universal corruption, which is swept away by the flood. After the deluge, there arises a period of universal pride, drawing down on earth another universal punishment, of which human language bears the indelible traces through all time. The rise of states and the foundation of empires is another well-marked epoch, succeeded by the rise, spread, and almost universal dominion of idolatry. Then follow dreams of world-wide conquest, and world-wide empire. Assyria, Persia, Greece, Rome, wear the tiara of empire; each in turn, rewarded with earthly dominion for earthly virtue, decays at last under its own vices, and sinks, in its fall, under the burthen of woe denounced by the voice of prophecy. When the last of ancient empires, having passed the zenith of its glory, is declining under the load of its corruption, Christianity introduces a new epoch, marked by a new struggle between good and evil. The world, redeemed by the blood of God, is regenerated by the blood of twelve millions of martyrs. At the close of the first epoch of Christianity, there is, beyond the boundaries of Roman civilization, a vast upheaving of barbaric nations, the barbarian awaking from his long slumber in the world, and rushing upon the empires of civilization to accomplish the will of God. It is the age of barbarian invasion. Scourges in the hands of God to chastise, and rend in pieces, corrupt, idolatrous, persecuting Rome—the Goth, the Hun, the Vandal issue from their trackless forests in the North of Europe. Armies of Mongols pour down from their mountain fastnesses in the far east of Asia. From the desert of Arabia the prophet of Mecca sends forth his hordes with scimitar and torch to subdue the finest, but most corrupt regions of Asia, Africa, Europe, to the sensual religion of the Koran. The epoch of barbarian invasion introduces a period strongly characterized by the conflict of new and old ideas and manners, of Roman and barbaric legislation, of the strong passions of the forest, and the effeminate polish of an effete civilization. Out of this vast chaos, gradually moulded into harmony by the action of religion, arises the brilliant empire of Charlemagne. Its dismemberment leads to feudalism, that mixed period of great vices, and splendid virtues, which, for four or five centuries, shaped the laws, manners, and ideas of European society. Feudalism gives birth to chivalry. It is the age of the Crusader, —the glorious age of Christian chivalry. Roused by a generous enthusiasm, the new nations of Europe gird on the heroic sword of the Crusader, in the holy cause of the rights of man, and the rights of heaven. Placing the cross upon their mailed armor, forgetting their ancient feuds, Frank, Lombard, Saxon, Norman, wave on wave, throng to glorious battle. Side by side, like brothers, the legions of the cross rush against the polluted and polluting legions of the crescent. All Europe, from the Mediterranean to the Baltic, resounds with the war cry, new in history, of "God wills it," "God wills it." The latter portion of the Middle Ages, now thoroughly civilized by the persevering action of the church, lays the foundation of our Modern Progress. It is a brilliant period of art. Christian architecture builds the lofty aisle and soaring pinnacle of the Gothic Cathedral; Christian painting adorns the majestic pile with masterpieces of spotless purity, and awe-inspiring grandeur. The Middle Ages close with an epoch of peaceful, but mighty revolutions. It is an age of artistic and literary revolution: an age of discovery and invention. The art of painting, the discovery of a new world, the revival of letters, change the current of all events, and remodel the whole of the future history of man. Upon the threshold of modern history, corruption, grown up amid the splendor of discovery and the classic beauty of arts and letters, causes the universal cry of Reform, characteristic of the sixteenth century. It is an epoch of Religious revolutions. Nations, forgetting to reform their own corrupt manners, attempt to change what the Eternal had founded to last unchangeably through all time. Then follow for long years, the combined scourges of war and tyranny, two of the heaviest scourges which the Almighty in His wrath can send to chastise the world. The spirit of liberty, the characteristic spirit of the eighteenth century, protests against the absolutism sprung out of the Reformation. It is an age of political Revolutions. The spirit of liberty, thrilling the nations from Europe to America, founds on our own shores the glorious republic of George Washington. In Europe, perverted by the evil genius of infidelity, it ends in the dark days of the French Revolution. It calls up from its own bosom the scourge of its excesses. Its children are led to useless slaughter, in myriads on myriads, by the mighty but tyrannic genius of Bonaparte.

Opening amid the storms of revolutionary battles, offspring of an age of revolutions which have changed the whole aspect of civilized society, itself the parent of new revolutions in art, science, commerce, industry, our age opens a new era in the history of the world. Its characteristic spirit sums up the characteristics of all ages. Its motto is Universal Progress. More widely, more deeply swayed by a common impulse than any period which has preceded it, claiming as its own, every name expressive of Progress, proudly boasting itself an age of freedom and independence, an age of light,—attempting at times to carry its ruling spirit of Progress to the very heart and the very altars of God; our age, according as truth or error, virtue or vice inspires its prevailing spirit, must rise to unequalled glory, or descend to unequalled shame, merit heaven's blessings in overflowing measure, or deserve vials filled with darkest vengeance. This consequence is evident from all history; it would be easy to demonstrate it from the very nature of things; it is strikingly illustrated by the history of single individuals, endowed with extraordinary powers, and bending all their energies to effect their objects.

Such men, angels in human form, or incarnate spirits of evil, are the towering figures of history, the saviours or destroyers of the world. They are conquerors like Cyrus and Alexander; scourges like Atilla and Ghengis Khan; patriots like Washington; they are legislators like Solon and Lycurgus; they are discoverers like Columbus; they found philosophic schools like Plato and Aristotle; they are apostles like St. Paul and St. Francis Xavier; founders of religious orders like St. Dominic and St. Benedict; or dark religious innovators like Mahomet and Luther; or fierce enemies of religion and morals like Voltaire and Rousseau. Indeed, in any sphere, the power of single men is often wide as the world, boundless as truth or error, enduring like time. Such men alter the boundaries of empire and 'the destinies of nations. They change realms into deserts, or deserts into blooming fields. They create armies of widows and orphans, or make all generations debtors to their burning charity and holy zeal. They stem the current of error, or extend it like a flood. They transform the votaries of Venus into martyrs, or the sons of martyrs into slaves of sensuality. They mould the character of their own time, leave their impress on all history, and for weal or woe, for time and eternity, influence the lot of countless millions of their fellow beings.

These facts form a startling illustration of what may be expected when the whole civilized world, with all its varied energies, moves under the impulse of a common spirit; when it employs its millions of mighty arms, tasks all its treasures of genius, wealth, power, to accomplish a single work. This, to an extent unprecedented in history, our age has done, and is doing. Conscious of its unsurpassed resources, proud of its triumphs in art and science, it has attempted with unexampled determination, to eclipse all by-gone ages. It moves, like a disciplined army, under one banner, the banner of universal progress. Here, too, lies its danger. There is alike ground for fear and hope. The inheritor of all that is great and glorious, of all that is ignoble and degraded in the past, it bears in its bosom the germ of all human greatness, the principles of all human degradation. It may adopt the disorganizing doctrines bequeathed to it. It may choose to follow the eternal light of truth, which forms the strength and safety of nations and of the world. It may improve on the vices which have ruined ancient societies. It may emulate the virtues of the most heroic times. It may fall from ruin to ruin, or rise from glory to glory. It may end in unparalleled disasters; it may close in peerless grandeur.

Hence the various opinions which men have formed of this Age of Progress, its tendencies, its history, its destinies. What has it effected? Whither is it hastening? Some, looking only at the bright side of things, are disposed to rank it higher than the greatest in the past, and to predict for it a future of ever increasing greatness. Theirs is the poet's motto:

"Time's noblest offspring is the last."

Others turning to the dark side of the picture, regard it as one of the worst of ages, and think they see the future looming up from our own vices like a lowering tempest: the future to them appears pregnant with calamity.

Time will not allow me this evening to discuss the whole question here presented. I shall limit myself in this lecture to a historical sketch of the age, reserving for the next a more detailed examination of its danger. An impartial review of what the age has accomplished, will enable us to judge how far it is really entitled to the name of Age of Progress; while the study of its dangers, may, perhaps, enable us to foresee how far we may expect a repetition of the ruin denounced against all nations who forget their God. The two lectures form parts of but one whole, which, I hope, will justify, in some degree, the long preliminary remarks in which I have indulged.

In attempting to delineate this Age of Progress, as it is, I must necessarily confine myself to a few prominent facts, a mere outline, the details of which fill our modern libraries, are daily multiplied by what passes around us, and recorded as they occur in the ten thousand works, in all languages, yearly issuing from our prolific press.

The history of the Age, from the stand point of progress, may be reviewed in three different lights, corresponding to the three kinds of progress which it is possible for man to make, viz.: Intellectual Progress, Material Progress, Moral Progress.

In regard to Intellectual Progress, our age is chiefly marked by its advance in the natural sciences, and their application to the purposes of industry and commerce. In the domain of the natural sciences, it is clearly entitled to be called the Age of Progress. It stands at the head of Ages. It has perfected what former times only began. Out of the accumulated materials gathered by past labors it has erected a multitude of new sciences, while its own resources are preparing materials for still newer sciences. It is scarcely more than half a century since Chemistry, Mineralogy, Botany, Geology, and numerous other branches of natural history, became sciences really worthy the name. Many of the properties and laws of matter, it is true, were known in the most remote ages. The Alchymist, among the Arabians and Christians, in his anxious search of centuries after the elixir of life, and the mysterious stone whose touch was to transmute base metals into silver and gold, had brought up from the dark depths of nature a large number of important chemical secrets. The vast animal remains in the rocky strata which form the mountain side or protrude above the plain; the huge bones dug out from the field, or raised from the marsh, had, for upwards of two thousand years, given rise to geological speculations, to cosmological systems, sometimes extravagant, sometimes making surprising approximations to the truth. Solomon, the Scripture informs us, " treated about trees from the cedar that is in Libanus, unto the hyssop that cometh out of the wall."\* The sciences which may have been contained in the lost works of the wisest of men, were again investigated, at later periods, by such men as Aristotle, Theophrastus, Pliny ; and in the last century were partially revived by the labors of Linnaeus, Buffon, Lacepède, and others. But with the exception of Physics and Astronomy, scarcely one of all the branches of the natural sciences, had been placed on a scientific basis, at the opening of this century.

At the dawn of this century, amid the shock of political convulsions, amid the wreck of thrones and old political fabrics, science was silently working a revolution far mightier and far more enduring than any revolution wrought by the conspirators of '89, or by the brilliant sword of Bonaparte ; a revolution which changed for all time the commerce, the industry, the social intercourse, the wants, the ideas, the manners of nations. In their

\* Kings iv., 33.

religious bearings, the sciences of our age have vindicated the wisdom of that God whom infidel revolutionists in the last century imagined they had deposed from his Eternal throne. They have justified the records of that divine revelation which the cynical patriarchs of infidelity had cast away with triumphant scorn. I can do little more than allude to what has been accomplished.

The earliest of the new sciences, Chemistry, founded, as a science, at the close of the last century, by the genius of Lavoisier,\* has since obtained its most brilliant success. The cabalistic formulas, and mystic nomenclature of the alchymist, his cheerless groping in the dark, rarely catching a few glimpses of light, and ending after a life-time of labor in gloomy disappointment, are permanently replaced by scientific terminology, clear arrangement of facts, invariable laws, sure processes, clearly calculated results, intelligent foresight advancing with firm step to the discovery of new secrets. The brilliant experiments of modern chemistry, its power over the combinations of matter, its masterly analysis, its manifold applications to medicine, agriculture, industry; the invention of Daguerre, that beautiful, though familiar gift of chemistry,

---

\* Lavoisier died 1794 on the scaffold.

causing a ray of light to draw a portrait with a minuteness of perfection which no human hand can hope to equal; photography, delineating upon a piece of glass no larger than a pin's head, a landscape, a group of figures, a poem, which to the naked eye looks a mere black speck, but appears complete under the glass, with every trait and line sharply defined and exquisitely finished; or, in its recent application to astronomy, settling questions which had long divided the minds of the learned; all this, which has become so common that we have ceased to admire it, would have appeared a chimera, had it been predicted a hundred years ago; all this forms in reality one of the most striking triumphs which the human mind has obtained over the secrets of nature, even in this age of scientific triumphs. In a religious point of view, chemistry, proving that all compound substances in nature are combined according to invariable weight and measure, beautifully illustrates the text of wisdom, "Thou hast ordered all things in weights, and number, and measure." The grand discoveries of Galileo, Kepler, Newton, revealed the laws which rule the heavens; chemistry descending to the depths of the elements, counting and weighing the atoms, has revealed in the obscurest paths of nature an order, an economy, no less wonderful than the order and the harmony of the stars and planets; it has revealed in the *crystal* the same design as in the *blazing* orb; it has laid open another portion of that Sovereign wisdom and power, which holds atoms bound to atoms, as it holds world to world enchained in their mighty course through the bright immensity of the universe. This indeed is one of the noblest offerings made by science on the altar of revealed religion. Geology, Zoology, Botany, and other kindred sciences sprang up together about the beginning of this century; they have progressed together, each throwing light upon the other, while each advanced in its own sphere.

In 1800, Cuvier * announced to the scientific world a new science relating to fossil remains, in which he displayed a genius equal to the greatest that adorn the annals of the natural sciences. He relied in his researches on the constancy of the laws which God has established in the animal as in the mineral kingdom; on the unchangeable relation of the organs, their unvarying adaptation, each to each, and to the climate, food, habits of each species in the animal creation. Aided by his unrivalled

* In his first memoir on fossil Elephants. Cuvier, born in 1765, died in 1832.

knowledge of comparative anatomy he was able, from the structure of a single bone, dug up by chance from the sea beach or the field, and regarded by the ignorant as a portion of the skeleton of some extinct race of giants, to describe the whole structure of an animal, though every living individual of the species had long since vanished from the earth. He could describe its form, its size, its habits, its food, its haunts. His descriptions were so exact, that in many instances, they were verified by the subsequent discovery of entire skeletons. From the evidences of design which nature now exhibits, he succeeded in inferring what it was, in those obscure epochs, when the Mastodon and Deinotherium, the Ammonite and Nummulite sullenly walked the chaotic earth, or swarmed in the widely heaving waters of the primeval seas.

Ehrensberger,* a Prussian naturalist, examined the minuter forms. By the aid of the microscope he discovered that the animalculæ,—infusoria, as they are called,—of which as many as 500,000,000 may exist in a single drop of water, are not, as had been until then supposed, mere living specks of inorganized matter, but beings endowed with perfect organization. He found

* Born 1795.

that like the higher animals, they possess organs of sight, muscles, nerves, teeth, or at least, as subsequent researches have fully established, an organic structure, as wonderful as that of the huge elephant which swallows them by millions of millions in the running brook. These animalculæ, as diversified in their forms and habits, as bird, fish, or beast, furnish still another illustration of that infinite Power which shapes with equal ease the vast form of the Mastodon and perfect organisms more minute than the mote which sparkles in the sunbeam.

The same Prussian naturalist discovered that these minute forms of life have left, all over the earth, remains incomparably more extensive than those left by the higher species of extinct animals. His researches show that the soil which supports the forest, the quarry out of which palaces are built, are in many instances, but vast cemeteries, all made up of the microscopic remains of infusoria. The shields or skeletons of these animalculæ, consisting of solid silica or flint, of lime, of iron ore,* and often constituting nearly the whole of immense beds of rock, and vast fields of clay many feet in thickness, are of such extreme minuteness, that it takes from 30 to

* Oxide of iron.

40,000 millions of them to make up a single cubic inch. It has lately been found that the process which deposited these microscopic forms of life is still going on beneath the ocean. A few years ago,* the American expedition which sounded the Telegraphic Plateau, brought up from the bottom of the Atlantic, what appeared to the naked eye a mere mass of soft loam, but when subjected to the glass by the late Prof. Bailey, of West Point, proved to be a collection of shells, of exquisite mould. This discovery revealed the fact, that the waters of the ocean, like the waters of our brooks and rivers, swarm with microscopic life. The minute remains, gradually, softly sinking, like flakes of snow, have lined the whole surface of the ocean-bed with a downy covering of extinct life, and are renewing in its dark caves the first steps in the process which created the rock beneath our feet.

The ultimate purposes for which God has so profusely scattered these minute forms of life, in the clear, cold depths of stream and ocean, where the unaided eye discovers no trace of their existence, have not been explained. They are as little known as the last reason, why he has studded the heavens with suns, which, to unassisted

* See Maury.

vision look like mere sparks. However the researches of Zoology, and similar researches in Botany, have disclosed a portion of the mystery. They have revealed a new evidence of design, where formerly the plan of creation seemed less complete. They have made it clear that, in the animal and vegetable worlds, there exists, link on link, a complete chain of beings, from the microscopic mosses and algae to the gigantic palm tree; from the almost imperceptable minuteness of organization in the infusoria, to the exuberant muscular organism of the mammoth; just as faith reveals, in the world of intelligences, another chain of beings, extending from man through all the bright hierarchies of heaven, up to the highest seraph that burns before the throne of God.

The discoveries of Botany, Geology, Chemistry, and other kindred sciences, have likewise enabled Geology to base its theories on truly scientific principles. Geology, as a science, belongs entirely to this century. Its object is the *history* of the mineral masses of the globe and their organic remains. It counts and measures the rocky strata which form the outer crust of the earth. It investigates the forces which have lifted the enormous mountain chain, and filled with metallic deposits the fissures opened by the earthquake. In the interior of the rock, it studies the foot-prints, made when the unwieldy creatures described by Cuvier formed the earth's inhabitants. In the rock, on the mountain side, it interrogates the wave-lines, made by the tide, which rippled to the breeze, or rolled in the tempest, ere our present continents were heaved out of the ocean. It asks how many ages were required to prepare the coal-mine and the quarry and the rich soils above them; how many ages each family of extinct beings must have existed, when the remains of the little nummulite have sufficed to build pyramids; at what period in the changes of our globe, the Himalayas and the Andes were upheaved by the central forces of the earth, and golden sands were deposited at the foot of the snowy mountains, and in every El Dorado from the Ural to the plains of Australia. Many of these obscure problems, Geology fails to answer; many of its theories are still unsettled; but it has proved that, unless we wish to assert causeless miracles, we are forced by the obvious appearances of nature, to admit, before the creation of Adam, not literally six *days*, but *periods* whose enormous duration can only be counted by myriads of centuries.

In opening these magnificent views of preadamitic

periods receding in the dimness of the past beyond the present possibility of calculation, geology has rendered an important service to revealed religion. It has presented upon the book of Genesis, a commentary as splendid as it was unexpected. As far back as the fifth century of our era, St. Augustine had pointed out, that it was scarcely possible to take the first verses of Genesis in their literal meaning; for, he observed, the first Mosaic days could not have been days like ours, since there was neither sun nor moon to measure their duration. God, indeed, might have created the world in an instant, with all its appearances of remote antiquity; but the Scripture represents God as proceeding gradually; the spirit of God as moving over the dark waters of the primeval chaos; as bringing out, one by one, from its confused and jarring elements, each of the varied harmonies of earth and heaven, until the whole harmonious magnificence of the universe was completed, and the Eternal rested from all the works which his hand had made. In attempting to interpret what is so briefly and so mysteriously intimated in Holy Writ, Geology has adopted various theories, too numerous for present discussion. But whether the days stand for periods, or the mysterious Bereshith, "In the beginning," is meant to express indefinite duration, the general view presented by geology is in the highest degree worthy of God's eternal wisdom, and completely accordant with his eternal love for man. He whose counsels are coeval with his being; before whose boundless duration all time is but a passing day; before whose uncreated light all worlds are but a faint fleeting shadow, and man a mere speck in his infinitude, might well allow long ages to prepare man's dwelling. For man, though so lowly, he had loved even from *eternity*, as the masterpiece of his own hands. Though scarce worthy, he had destined him to live in beatific vision with his own eternal Being.

While Geology and other branches of natural history have received a scientific form, the other sciences have been advancing to perfection.

To cite but one instance, Astronomy. Though its cultivation began some three or four thousand years ago, under the clear Chaldean skies, though it was long since raised to the condition of an exact science by the genius of Kepler and Newton, it has yet obtained in this century some of its most brilliant successes. The great work of Laplace, La Mècanique Cèleste,* in which he traces out

* 1799-1825.

the law of universal gravitation in all its complicated influences, would alone suffice to render our age forever illustrious in the annals of Intellectual Progress. In 1801, while the first portion of this splendid work was going through the press, the accidental discovery of a small planet between the orbits of Mars and Jupiter, led to the discovery of a large series of asteroids,* the list of which is still steadily increasing. In close proximity to each other, these miniature planets have suggested the idea that they are only the *shattered fragments* of a large *planetary world*, and may ultimately furnish the means of demonstrating that, in *remote* epochs, those silent worlds blazing nightly over our heads, the image of unchangeable order, were subject to convulsions even more violent than those which have left their vast traces in our own globe. But the great triumph of our age, indeed, of any age, is the discovery of the planet Neptune. In 1781, Sir Wm. Herschel had discovered Uranus by accident. In 1846, Le Vernier in France and Adams in England, relying on the constancy of the laws of the heavens for their sole guide, discovered, by mere *arithmetical* calculation, the spot where an additional planet was required by the solar

* 1801-1807; 1845.

system. The powerful telescope of Dr. Galle of Berlin, was turned to that spot, and near it blazed the mighty planet, an everlasting monument to the genius of scientific progress. This achievement, extraordinary as it is, scarcely surpasses Bessel's measurement of the distance of the fixed stars from the sun; a problem which had long baffled all the efforts of Astronomy, and, indeed, had been thought incapable of solution. This was in 1838. Science has begun to sound the farthest depths of the heavens, as it is endeavoring to penetrate the obscure depths of preadamitic ages. Bessel's measurements show that it takes light, moving at the rate of 12,000,000 miles a minute, or 192,000 in a second, 45 years to reach our eyes from the polar star. To reach one of the nearest of the fixed stars (61 Cygni,) it would take a rail-car traveling night and day, at the rate of 20 miles an hour, 324,000,000 of years. In 1803, Sir Wm. Herschel's discovery of Binary Stars, that is, of systems composed of two stars, each revolving around the other in regular orbits, furnishes good grounds for the conviction that the entire universe is made up of systems of suns, many of them incomparably brighter than our own.* Each of these Solar worlds appears to move with

\* Dr. Wollaston.

its train of planets around a common centre, probably Alcyone,* the central star in the Pleiades. It has been calculated that our own world, our great sun,† with all its glorious planetary orbits, with all its circling comets, is carried forward, in its motion around the Great Central Sun of the universe, towards some point in the constellation Hercules,°‡ at the rate of 154,000,000 of miles a year.

These efforts, made to ascertain the laws of the heavens, are equalled by the efforts made of late years to ascertain the laws which govern climates, the fixed laws which rule the ever changing influence of heat, light, electricity, magnetism, on land, on sea, in the atmosphere. From these endeavors, an entirely new science is springing up, known under the general name of meteorology; it is an attempt to map the course of the winds and clouds across the sky, to track the hurricane in its devastating path, to mark the undulating line of climates around the globe, to fix the subtile laws followed by the fluctuating and changeful directions of the magnetic and electric currents. This scientific undertaking, the most unpromising perhaps ever

---

\* Maedler.     † 1783-1805-1806.
° Sir Wm. Herschel.   ‡ In a line joining the two stars n & u Herculis. (Vide the Prussian Astronomer Struve.)

entered upon by man, has already produced such works as Maury's celebrated Geography of the Sea; it has in part *mapped* the winds, it has shortened the mariner's path across the trackless ocean, traced the laws by which the currents of the ocean are made to carry the warmth of the tropics to the north-western shores of Europe and America.

These proofs of scientific progress might be indefinitely multiplied, by instances drawn from other sciences, such as Hydrodynamics, Optics, and other branches of Physics; or from Ethnology, Philology and the recent researches in Archeology, Geography, History; all of which, time compels me to pass by in silence. It would require volumes to enumerate every invention, every improvement, in every species of scientific progress, made in the last fifty years. I can only allude, in passing, to those glorious historical researches, which, as in the case of Hurter's life of Innocent III, have vindicated the names of great Pontiffs, defamed by ages of calumny.

Could we dwell on the fine arts, we should find sculptors, painters, architects, such as would have done honor to the age of Leo X; in literature, poets whom the age of Pericles would have been proud to own; orators, whose voice, like that of Demosthenes could rouse nations, and make tyrants tremble. Indeed, our age has produced a man who, as an orator, stands alone, and whose name is justly enshrined in the hearts of a people as glorious for their constancy, as their persecutors are infamous for three centuries of cruelty. Demosthenes could terrify Philip, he could not prevent the subjugation of Greece; O'Connell, at the head of a down-trodden people, made England quail, and relax for a moment her tyrannic grasp. The annals of political eloquence, either in our own or any other age, offer no example of a triumph like that gained by the eloquence of Daniel O'Connell when he wrenched from the blood-stained hand of England the first reluctant instalment of long-deferred justice, which unbound one chain from the neck of the down-trodden,— the act of Catholic Emancipation. His name, by the memories it awakens, by the holy cause of which it is the symbol, by the great triumph it commemorates, forms an epoch in the story of Ireland's wrongs, an epoch in Christian history, another glory for the Isle of Saints, an immortal honor to the human race.

But though eloquence, poetry, art have produced great geniuses, still it must be owned that, on the whole, as an artistic and literary age, our century can not rank with the ages of Pericles, Augustus, or Leo X. The claim of our age to be regarded as an age of Intellectual Progress, lies mainly in its progress in the natural sciences. In this respect, indeed, it stands at the head of all ages.

With the characteristic spirit of the age, with its immense activity, its boldness, its originality, its indomitable perseverance, drawing forth energy from reverses, it is impossible to assign limits to the progress which may be made even before this century closes. From the Cape of Good Hope to St. Petersburg, from Washington to Madras, from a hundred observatories, the sleepless watch-towers of science, the astronomer nightly turns his powerful glass to the blue deep of the heavens, and seeks to penetrate still farther the mysteries infolded in their azure depths. On land, in the city, in the country, out on the desert plain, the meteorologist notes each fitful change of the elements. On sea, under every sky, a thousand mariners lend their aid to the advancement of the new science, and record each breath of wind that fills their sails, each current that alters their course, each passing cloud that obscures the sun. To extend the field of the natural sciences, there are men who brave the deadly cold of the Polar night, and the deadly heat of the African sun. Under the grasp of powerful minds in every country, each discovery is made to supply new means of investigation, each new science made a power capable of disclosing new secrets. Far as man may reach, there are always farther depths in nature. While one enigma is solved, glimpses are caught of darker riddles. The profound sciences of nature's laws are offered by the Almighty as perpetual food to the unceasing activity of the human mind. Though the laws and properties of matter are limited, man cannot reach their last limit. The created can never master the last secret of the Creator.

The obvious inference is, that the natural sciences, are, in their very essence, progressive. The spirit of Scientific Progress, if it continue for a hundred years, may produce an epoch to which our times shall appear like an age of Science in its infancy,—like the gray dawn to the full blaze of noonday.

Still our age will always be known as an age of great scientific progress. What it has done, will ever entitle it to the grateful remembrance of posterity. Even Revealed Religion, as I have remarked, has cause to thank it. I know that a modern reviewer of great name,* in speaking of the connection of science with *natural* religion remarks that "the discoveries of modern Astronomers and Anatomists have really added nothing to the force of that argument which a reflecting mind finds in every beast, bird, insect, fish, leaf, flower and shell." True, they have added nothing to the substantial strength and logical completeness of the argument, but they have added to its authentic completeness and moral beauty. Each new discovery of Science is a trophy, with which Religion loves to adorn her altars. To the rudest minds, it is true, the universe breathes and speaks of God. To the rudest of ages, heaven and earth were eloquent instructors. Ere one natural science was founded, ere one law of the stars was known, the ever returning, ever fresh fertility of spring, the teeming earth exhaling fragrance from fruit and flower, —the burnished insect buzzing in the sunbeam,—the huge beast filling the forest with his yell,—the loud voice of thunder,—the sublimity of the wide ocean,—the tempest raging on the deep,—the mimic murmur of the

* Macaulay, in Ranke's Hist. of the Popes 36, Edin. Rev., Oct., 1840.

glossy spiral shells on the sea-beach,—the unfading beauty of the heavens and the many twinkling golden stars,—the sun daily running his unerring career,—all nature, with its mysterious laws of inert matter and organized existence,—life, motion, feeling, mysteriously separated or mysteriously combined,—the universe, ever sublime in the immensity of its proportions, ever exquisitely beautiful in the perfection of its minutest parts,—all this, in all time, was all-sufficient to impress man with awe for the power, with love for the beneficence of the Great Creator. Upon all its ample vaults, and all its splendid decorations, the universe ever bears the stamp of infinite wisdom, and infinite power. But still, modern science, investigating and revealing many of the hidden laws of matter ; explaining the origin of the tempest and the voice of the storm ; discovering a world of organized life in a drop of crystal water,—generations of extinct life in the forest and the quarry; interrogating the mountain-side, and learning the secret history of the ages of the Creation ; attempting to measure the depths of the heavens, and discovering there the existence of millions of blazing worlds, scattered through all space beyond the possible discoveries of man— universe within universe, all moving in concentric union around a common sun; modern science, in all the vastness of the mysteries it has disclosed surely presents, far more eloquent views of God's glory, than the universe of itself would suggest. It gives rise to more awe-inspiring ideas of God's omnipotence; opens deeper abysses in his wisdom; endows the heavens with a new voice of praise. It allows us still to view this boundless world with its boundless history, as our own home. We may still view it as being merely a beautiful image of the boundless love of God for us—for you—for me, who though thus lost in our vast home, like mere motes unseen in the sunbeam—a nothing in the immeasurable expanse of God's creation—are yet, small as we are, the masterpieces of God's own hand, the grand object of the most loving care of our Great Creator.

These reflections are obvious, but they are not the ordinary view which the age takes of our Intellectual Progress. Our age may boast its broad systems of education, its universal diffusion of intelligence; but it has no peculiar title to be called a religious age, or an age of faith. Its ruling spirit is rather the spirit of material progress. To this our great Intellectual Progress is made subordinate and subservient. What our age demands of the natural sciences is to increase its wealth, to open new gold mines, to create new highways for commerce, to improve machinery, to invent new comforts, to create new luxuries.

Founded on our unparalleled progress in the natural sciences, our material progress has itself been unparalleled. Never, in all history, was any age distinguished like ours for brilliant applications of science to industry and commerce; for discoveries and inventions which have at once revolutionized all industrial pursuits, and the whole commercial intercourse of the civilized world. To enumerate every instance of material progress, would consume days and weeks, as witness the annual reports of our Patent Offices. The whole subject, indeed, is too generally known to require to be dwelled upon. Minor improvements are a matter of every day occurrence. The GREAT inventions have lost their novelty. We have become familiarized with the gigantic powers of the Steam Engine; we hardly notice the hum of the myriad wheels and levers it sets in motion; we are used to its rapid, finished workmanship, and its untiring energies;—the long train of men and merchandise, whirled across the continent; the boat breasting the rapid stream; the steamship battling with the tempest; all these have lost their sublimity. From sea to sea, lightning is our familiar messenger, it must soon enable Europe and America to communicate across the storms of the Atlantic. We have become accustomed to every new form of our material civilization; to new commercial ideas; to the intimate dependence of nation upon nation; to the general prosperity or distress produced in every quarter of the globe, by the prosperity or distress of a single country; to new social conditions of every description, created by new inventions. What would have appeared, a hundred years ago, as fabulous, as the visions of an Arabian tale, has become to us mere matter of fact. We have ceased to wonder at any of the effects of our material progress, however new in the history of the world. Yet, we may review all the social, industrial, commercial revolutions in the 6,000 years of human history, and we shall discover but *one* epoch which can at all be compared with ours. That single period we shall find at the close of those ages which it is the fashion of our day to stigmatize as Dark Ages. But in spite of sarcasm and contempt, it will remain true forever, that the genius of invention created the press under the influence of the old religion; the genius of discovery sailed to the shores of a new world, under the shadow of the cross; the sons of the Middle

Ages, nurtured in the old despised Religion, laid the foundation of our own progress; in their day they wrought social and commercial changes, almost as brilliant as our own, and more glorious because they had not forgotten to be grateful to that Church, whose action had raised the nations of Europe from barbarism to splendid civilization. Without her action we should, at this day, be wanderers in the forest, like our barbarian forefathers.

Our age forgets that gratitude is a duty. It likewise often forgets the miseries its spirit of Material Progress has engendered. Indeed when we look only at the surface of things, the glitter of our modern civilization appears so dazzling, that we are apt to overlook the dark scenes concealed beneath it. Yet the distress of the age, with all its varied forms of wretchedness presents a picture far more interesting in its sadness than the brightest page in the history of our Material or Intellectual Progress. But as the subject has been lately treated in this hall, I shall offer but one or two remarks upon it, to give some degree of completeness to this historical sketch of the Age of Progress.

The distress of our times has in great part arisen from our very Progress. The machine had replaced the arm of the laborer. In the older and more thickly settled countries, it has taken bread from the table, fuel from the hearth, cheerfulness from the wretched dwellings of thousands on thousands of families, once happy in the frugal enjoyment of the hard-earned fruits of daily labor. From the intimate commercial dependence of nations upon each other it has followed, that a revolution in one country stops the wheels of industry all over the civilized world, and carries famine to the cottage of the mechanic.

Modern progress has produced huge riches: it has likewise produced intense selfishness, a second great cause of distress. Selfishness alone is responsible for the existence of squalid want, famine and starvation, in the midst of plenty. It is because wealth has made men selfish, that we find, back of the street lined with palaces, where wealth lives in unpitying luxury, the crowded lane, the fetid court, the under-ground den, where haggard misery crouches in despair;—starvation the next neighbor to overgrown riches;—the earthen hovel open to the December blast, by the side of the palatial residence. The selfishness of wealth has invented the gloomy work-house, the prison of poverty, where the pauper, to escape starvation, must barter his liberty for a morsel of hard bread. In the English coal mine it allows the existence of still darker forms of wretchedness. Far away from the cheerful light of day, bent upon the mineral, degraded in its own estimation, extracting fuel for the wealthy manufactory,—down there in the deep, dark coal mine, there is a forgotten mass of human labor—there is the English Coal-digger, a species of wretch who has no equal in Christian lands, wearing away his miserable existence, from father to son, in ignorance whether Christ ever existed, seldom hearing the name of God—living and dying excluded even from the consolations of religion, the last comfort of human affliction.

These scenes of distress, exhibited by a land which claims to stand at the head of modern progress, may find a counterpart in other countries. To some extent, perhaps, selfishness may succeed in palliating their enormity. But there is another scene of unexampled wretchedness for which England's tyranny alone is responsible. She has granted Catholic Emancipation, but she exterminates the Catholic people. Near that same rich English isle is another island, rich by nature, doomed to hopeless misery. The teeming fields of

Ireland are the granary of England. Ireland's brave sons are the nerve of British armies, the bulwark of her empire. In her blind religious hatred, she calls Ireland prosperous when cattle have replaced the cottage, and entire villages are levelled by the crowbar, at the command of the merciless landlord. While she fattens on Ireland's wealth, she allows famine to decimate her population. While the luxuries of all her rich colonies are poured into her harbors, she allows the emigrant ship to sail forth loaded down with the victims of a famine, which her own exactions have created. If in one glance you would take in a scene of distress, such as no other age ever witnessed, look at the emigrant ship in years of famine, when its anchor is lifted, its white sails spread to the wind, and the exile of Erin bids farewell to his poor kindred, and the green fields of his unhappy country. On the shore there is a crowd of emaciated forms, gazing wistfully at the departing loved ones. They are too poor to fly from the inhospitable soil. Tyranny has doomed them to perish by the wayside. On deck there is a crowd, scarcely less wretched. There is the gray-haired sire trembling with age, casting, in speechless agony, a last glance at the home of his youth. There is the feeble mother, sobbing over her little ones, and perhaps peopling the unknown land with new oppressors, new persecutors, like those who have blighted her own. Follow the white sail across the Sea,—bearing off the load of so many broken hopes, so many withered affections; descend into the hold, fraught with fever, the home of death; listen to the loud, long wail of daily burial. The Ocean, from Liverpool to New York, is a wide grave for those poor children of oppression; the ooze of the Sea, for three thousand miles is decked with their whitening bones. No age has ever witnessed such a scene of sorrow. A society clad in silks, and broad-cloth, the great, the learned, the mighty, look on with cold indifference, or contemptuous disgust. It is much if they allow a foreign nation to freight a vessel with the alms which they refuse from their own overflowing coffers. Knowing that any year may bring back a repetition of the same harrowing scenes, they take no measure to mitigate the oppression which produced them. The victim departs and dies with a Christian's pardon, and a Christian's prayer for the nation that struck him down. But there is a God on high, who has heard every sigh, a God who has counted all the martyred dead. He, whose right hand destroyed all-ruling, persecuting Rome, has numbered the days of the persecutor. The hour must come, as it has come for all who have ever oppressed God's poor, when England, the proud mistress of the sea, she on whose world-encircling empire the sun forever shines, shall present in her world-wide wreck another moral to point another page in the dreadful history of persecutors. History shall point her finger to that wreck, and lifting her eye to heaven, say to the nations risen to greatness where England fell, Thus at last fall the mighty when they dare raise their hand against the Church of God, and trample upon the sorrows of the poor.

This single instance of Ireland's oppression would suffice to show that great as has been the Material Progress of the Age, Moral Progress forms no distinguishing characteristic even of a country most renowned for its material greatness. Indeed Moral Progress is not the characteristic of the age.

Here I feel that I am entering upon a difficult question. Has there been in the last fifty years any marked increase of crime? Is our age, all things considered, really worse than preceding ages? This question I shall not undertake to decide; but there are some forms of crime which appear to me to be decidedly peculiar to our age.

A spirit of lawless speculation, causing frequent revulsions of capital, general failures, universal distress; premeditated bankruptcies, entailing the ruin of orphans and widows, including the deliberate theft of the hard-earned wages of the laborer; such crimes among our forefathers would have been a topic of conversation for a life-time; among us they are so frequent, that the press has ceased to notice them, unless they are accompanied with some circumstances of startling enormity. Ordinary crimes of this nature are accomplished in forms which enable the criminal to escape the law, and live on respected as a man of honor.

Excessive love of wealth, the source of these crimes, deadens the heart to the influences of religion, and leads to infidelity. Infidelity may not be as loudly insolent now as it was in the last century, nor attack God with its old cynic contèmpt of public decency, but it has reproduced itself in forms peculiar to our age. It has given rise to revolutionary theories, aiming at the subversion of all government; to socialistic theories, attacking the foundation of property; to communistic theories, aimed at the destruction of the family; to materialistic theories, seeking the destruction of human dignity. Infidelity has gone so far as to teach that property is theft, vice is virtue, and God is evil.* These theories are proclaimed in open day, because amid a world, given up to self-interest, and grown half infidel, their authors scarcely find a manly voice to oppose them. They rely on the approval, and support of wretched masses of ill-rewarded, discontented labor. They rely on the ambition of demagogues, who, in times like ours, never want the will to kindle the spark of discontent into the flame of rebellion. Often brought up without religion, taught by the example of those above them to regard wealth as the chief good, there are armies among the wretched, ever ready to look on the rich as criminals, and to hold all government unjust which does not place wealth, or at least bread, in their own hands. Conspiracy finds its natural food in the dark lane, the cold garret, the damp cellar. There crime festers in its rags; there murder learns its trade in

---

\* "God is but folly and timidity; God is but hypocrisy and deceit; God is but tyranny and misery; God is evil."
Proudhon, System of Contradictions, C. VIII.
(Ap. Cortes, B. II. C. I., p. 184.)

"The true remedy against fanaticism . . . . is to prove to humanity that God, if he exists, is its enemy."
Id. Ibid., (Ap. Cortes, p. 179.)

sullen silence. There, back of the palace, grows up a society nurtured to hatred, awaiting its hour to wreak merciless vengeance on those who trample on their helplessness. There Red-Republicanism recruits its ranks; there is the standing menace to European society ; there the focus of those frequent commotions, whose temporary excesses portend what they will accomplish, when all the flood-gates of hoarded hatred are opened. Red-Republicanism is a spirit as fierce as that which changed France, but little more than fifty years ago, into a den of wild anarchy, where the passions of the atheist glutted themselves with the blood of the best men; where a mob, drunk with the blood of new martyrs, worshiped a naked outcast as the goddess of reason, and saluted the guillotine as the redeemer of the nation. That spirit is the standing menace of European society ; it is at the root of the great social evil of Europe, the permanent revolutionary state, the great socialistic conspiracy, necessitating, in times of apparently profound peace, huge standing armies, to protect society against its own members. Often breaking through all restraints, inaugurating the reign of massacre, convulsing nations, displacing dynasties, it forces the best portions of European communities to look forward to the future with dismal forebodings; it makes the wisest feel as if they lived in a land of earthquakes and volcanoes, not knowing whether the morrow's sun will not rise on a world of anarchy, above which Red-Republicanism shall be seen to wave its bloody hand, the signal of a new Reign of Terror.

Infidelity, likewise, is at the root of the Italian secret society; it inspires its horrid oaths, its hatred of religion, its hypocrisy putting on, at need, the mask of piety; it breathes the spirit of midnight assassination; it nerves the hand that plies the dagger in the dark; it presides at the midnight conventicle, where conspiracy learns the art of murder from the art of the surgeon. Fiercely determined to subvert religion, by subverting morality, it labors to corrupt the morals of the nations by poisoning the morals of youth. When its hour of triumph came, in 1848, it invented the well known horrid rites, and prompted the vile orgies of the Italian revolution. The same spirit, invading monarchs, has made them wage war for an *idea*, which was a lie to justice. It has led them to wage war for the Mahometan: to sacrifice for the maintenance of Turkish power, the lives of the sons of the Crusaders. At Naples it made sworn ministers betray their sovereign—the youthful, chivalrous, brave Francis. Ingrained hypocrites, they sapped their country's strength, while pretending to build up its power. When their plot was ripe, and the hordes of Garibaldi had landed in Calabria, they gave up their own country, bound hands and feet, to the tender mercies of a ruffian soldiery, collected from all the sewers of European depravity. About the same time, we beheld another novel spectacle of consummate hypocrisy, only matched by its subsequent unexampled effrontery. We beheld Piedmont, at first in secret league with the red-shirt of the revolution, and the murderous stiletto of the Carbonari, attacking Naples and the Sovereign Pontiff in the disguise of friendship; then throwing off the mask, and avowing their alliance, in her impudent trust that a corrupt public opinion would applaud her; lending open aid to Garibaldi to despoil the Venerable Pontiff of his small possessions, outraging her own Catholic people, and insulting for years the loudly declared sentiments of 200,000,000 of men, who regard Pius IX. as the representative of Christian civilization, cling to him as the centre and bulwark of Christian faith, revere him as the heaven-appointed vice-gerent of God.

Springing from corruption, Infidelity leads to worse

corruption. We owe to it, in our own country, that monstrous birth Mormonism, a new Mahometanism sprung from the infidel corruption of our civilization—as the old Mahomet sprung from the infidel corruption of the Arabian desert—looming up in the heart of the country, as a nation within a nation, with a code of laws whose basis is immorality, with a religion whose essence is combined vice and impiety.

Demon-worship is another monstrous offspring of the same prolific parent. Demon-worship, expelled 1800 years ago, has re-appeared under the form of spiritism, and re-awaked the very spirit of ancient oracles, long silenced by the voice of the Gospel. The medium replaces the Pythoness, the spirit-meeting stands for Delphi and Dodona. Spiritism, starting up in an obscure corner, spreading over the world like a plague, still maintaining its empire, far and wide, though just now public attention is withdrawn from it by more absorbing events, has given cause to dread that a large portion of civilized society is ready to relapse into some new and threatening form of paganism.

Infidelity serves to explain several other species of crime existing among us. It explains our marked recklessness of human life; the exquisite forms of treachery often starting out of the polish of our manners, like hideous asps darting out of the smooth green-sward; startling apparitions of corruption occasionally rising up from among the higher ranks of life, rending the veil, disclosing unknown depths of depravity underlying the surface of our civilization, proving that morality is undermined, and leaving us in suspense whether or not we should regard the splendor of our material progress, as forming but a brilliant covering of a darkly heaving mass of unrevealed corruption.

This much, however, is certain, that the spirit of infidelity sprung from corruption, has undertaken to complete the corruption. It proposes to educate youth without religion, to support government without morality, society without God. Scorning all religion, the determined and eternal enemy of God and man, wherever it exists, it enkindles the spirit of religious persecution. A traitor at heart to all government, of which it saps the two-fold foundation, Religion and morals, it accuses those who worship God and obey his Church, of hostility to the land of their birth or the land of their adoption. It continues the history of its pagan prototype.

Of old, no calamity could befal the Roman empire, but the infidel rabble of Rome, would shout with all its voices. "The Christians to the lions." Let a calamity befall a country in our day, and our *infidel press* will discover that Catholics are at the root of the evil, which their own hypocritic fanaticism may have in part occasioned. Does it not rise here—did it not rise shortly after the Mexican Campaign—where Catholic blood was poured out like water, to uphold the honor of the Stars and Stripes—did it not rise in all its cynic impudence, take its stand upon the piles of our dead heaped upon every bloody battle-field, and tell the country North and South, East and West, that Catholics, forsooth, are the eternal enemies of the republic for which they die! Here, as in Italy, it loves the mid-night conventicle—it takes secret oaths, for purposes which it has not the manliness to avow to the world. It invades the Sanctuary of Virgins consecrated to God; it arms the convent-burner with a torch—it organizes the Know-Nothing Massacre. Its history is written in the ruins of Charlestown, and in the blood-stained streets of Louisville. Let a war break out in any portion of the world, it will keep aloof from danger, when the voice of its bleeding country implores its aid; it will gloat over the terrors of the contest while blood will aid to fill its coffers—infidelity, a living vampire, feeding and fattening on the generous dead.

I might proceed further in the history of the crimes of our Age of Progress, but I shall have occasion to return to this subject in the last lecture of this course. Let us turn for a moment to a more cheerful theme.

Our age, indeed, is an age of extraordinary contrasts. Side by side with the triumphs of scientific invention, rise the triumphs of infidelity; unprecedented miracles of progress, are deformed by deeds of monstrous iniquity. Our exuberant wealth brings out but the more darkly the gloomy outlines of overwhelming distress.

Our age has produced, flourishing side by side with irreligion, vice, degradation—as the lily breathes in the same atmosphere with the thorn, the palm with the upas—a very harvest of purity, generosity, lofty heroism, martyrdom, which in the eye of high Heaven renders this sad earth still lovely, still worthy of the angels' smile, still deserving of God's choicest benedictions.

Charity, leaning over the plague stricken; charity, amid the storm of battle, peacefully bending over the dying soldier; charity, in the calm purity of the cloister, laboring in silence to redeem the poor, cast-off child of sin; charity, replacing a mother's affection, around the hearth of the orphan; charity, in the garb of the Little Sister of the Poor, going through the driving winter's sleet, to knock at the gates of wealth, and beg in the name of Christ a crust of daily bread, for a poor suffering brother: all this you have heard extolled with matchless eloquence; all this you may witness daily and hourly; all this magnificence of virtue is so common even in our age, that you will scarcely find more numerous examples of it in the heroic ages of Christianity.

The ancient, venerable church does not grow old. Loaded with eighteen centuries of honor, she is fresh as when she sprang, in heavenly beauty, from the hands of her divine founder. "Time writes no wrinkle on her *immortal* brow." Now, as ever, He whose life is her life, redeems the world. Still, as in her early days, amid the foul corruption of pagan Rome, she produces holiness and purity, which make men say, "Behold, she is the Church of God." And the learned of England, and the proudest and haughtiest of all nations, come from heresy, come from infidelity, come from paganism, come to her

# THE AGE OF PROGRESS. 57

and fall at her feet, and seek from her the life that vivifies the world.

Around the ruined thrones of Kings, whose mad conspiracies, in the last century, had nearly broken up the sources of Catholic Missions, the spirit of Apostleship has revived with its ancient ardor. In the palm groves of India, the successors of DeBritto combat the cruel pantheism of the Brahmin. The inheritors of the spirit of Xavier take up his labors among the sons of his fervent converts in the kingdom of Travancore. In China, the Apostle halts not timidly around bristling forts and armed shipping, with nations at his back to avenge his wrongs; but all alone, with the cross upon his cassock as his only armor, braving the cangue and the cage, he seeks to gather around the cross, which European valor has erected on the Cathedral of Pekin, the remnants of a hundred and fifty years of devotion. In Lassa, on the far borders of Thibet, he attacks in their stronghold, the prejudices of 3,000 years of superstition. On the threshold of Japan in the neighborhood of Sancian, memorable for similar devotion, he awaits the hour when commercial interests shall reopen the barriers which commercial avarice closed, and enable him to reap the rich harvests of faith promised by the blood of thirty thousand Japanese Martyrs. He follows the track of the explorer, and in the skull-paved halls of the King of Dahomey, he would gladly ransom with his blood the myriad victims of African despotism. From some forgotten Isle, embosomed in the Pacific, he leads to Europe, to the shrines of the Apostles, the converted sons of the cannibal chieftain. He follows the emigrant across the steppes of Russia, and the pampas of South America. He is on the banks of the Amazon, and at the head-waters of the Parana. He plants the cross above the wild gorges of the Andes, or carves it on the granite peak overlooking our great western Savannahs. At the sources of the Mississippi and Missouri, he seeks the Indian in his wigwam, or follows the Blackfoot in his hunt across the wintry plain, at the foot of the Northern Rocky Mountains. He is among the deadly lagoons of Guiana to receive the last breath of the political prisoner. A martyr to his zeal, or a martyr to his faith, falling by the sword of the mandarin, or by the heat of the marsh-fever, he continues the apostolic fervor of all ages, the combats of the Roman Amphitheatre, the martyr-spirit that regenerates the world.

In all ranks, the eye of religion still discovers hearts unmoved by the world's siren song, souls obedient to every holy impulse, generous hearts open to every want, bands of brothers united, heart and hand, in the holy crusade of charity. Need I name again the Society of St. Vincent de Paul? Need I tell again of men of rank and influence, moved by the same holy devotion in Europe and America, making it a law of their lives to visit the poor man's dreary cabin, and sanctify their own lives by bringing joy to the fireside of forgotten suffering? Or need I name that glorious association of the Propagation of the Faith, an institution of our own age, wide as the world, gathering the widow's mite, as well as the rich man's offering, and with the united charities of all seeking to aid in kindling the torch of faith in the darkness of every heathen land? Or need I speak of that scarce less glorious Association of the Holy Childhood, that touching inspiration of the genius of charity in our age, redeeming with the alms of the little ones of Christian lands, the little ones whom the Chinese mother heartlessly throws by the wayside as fit food for dogs and swine? When future generations shall read the annals of this Age of Progress, they will linger with tears over the pathetic page telling of all these holy deeds, and deem it a brighter, because holier page, than all the bright rolls on which Material and Intellectual Progress shall emblazon their glories.

It would be an endless task to dwell on all the triumphs of Religion during the last sixty years. One more of these triumphs, in concluding, I cannot pass over without a brief notice. Three times in sixty years the sovereign Pontiff has been dragged or driven from the Quirinal. At this moment when kings have plundered him, and Piedmontese and Carbonari are quarrelling around the poor remnant of his small estate, the spontaneous devotion of the Catholic world has renewed the venerable old offering of Peter's Pence. A country still deeply Catholic, in spite of the wrongs committed in her name, France, forces her sovereign who has shown little zeal in the cause of the holy see, to stand guard at the palace gate of Pius IX, and ward off aggressors, even at the risk of falling by the revolutionary dagger. Faith may grow cold in the hearts of the many; in the souls of the few it burns with unwonted fires. The world, a few years since, witnessed the return of a species of devotion, so little known in modern times, that it seemed to belong, as their peculiar glory, to the chivalrous old Ages of Faith. Amid the attacks of new infidels, the spirit of ancient chivalry is suddenly rekindled. France, Belgium, Ireland, Spain, send forth to generous warfare the noblest sons of Europe. On the rock of Spoleto, on the plains of Castel Fidardo, in the Fortress of Ancona, if they could not conquer against overwhelming odds, they still offered an energetic protest, with their hearts' best blood, for truth against a lie, for outraged right and justice against hypocritic power. All honor to them, all honor to him the brave old African Chieftain, immortal Lamoriciere, the heroic leader of a heroic band, the Godfrey of a degenerate age. If his name, if their names, are not brightened with the halo of victory, they shall go down through all time radiant with the more glorious light of heroic devotion in one of the holiest causes in which a warrior ever drew his sword, or soldier ever shed his blood. While faithful history shall live, to speak of powers inventing hypocritic theories of non-intervention, or rejoicing with the joy of the ungenerous at the downfall of the helpless representative of 1800 years of Christian civilization, it will love to repeat how the brave fell nobly on the hopeless field of honor; how the spirit of chivalry redeemed, by its own unsullied sacrifice, a portion of the invader's shame. Remembered when the unholy bays of the conqueror have withered, and fallen to the dust; when national iniquity, applauded and exultant now, is judged and condemned; when the invader's sceptre has passed to other hands, and his throne to another dynasty; honored, when Garibaldi and Piedmont are brought to the pillory of the world's execration; honored, while a glow of manly enthusiasm can be kindled in a human breast, their names will awaken, in all coming generations, the response deserved by disinterested valor. And she, the great survivor of all ruins, and all iniquities, the immortal remembrancer of all good deeds, the church for whom they bled, will, in her ever youthful career through the ages, treasure their memories in her heart of hearts, among the holy recollections of her long life of warfare.

While such devotion remains on earth, crime cannot triumph altogether. The deeds, that would deface, in the eyes of posterity, the glories of our Intellectual and Material Progress; that would make the nineteenth century be known in history as an age, rich, it may be in inventions and discoveries, but dimmed by iniquities as enormous as its progress was splendid, will borrow from such devotion a lustre which envy cannot lessen, nor crime impair; which, like the mid-day sun hiding the broad spots upon its surface, will conceal, in its own pure splendor, much of the darkness of the age.

Ten thousand inventions will be forgotten. The most delicate wheel-work of our machinery may come to be despised as the gross handiwork of art in its infancy. The newness of discovery fades as it floats down the stream of time. The brilliancy of genius is overshadowed by more brilliant genius; progress obscured by brighter progress. The voice of the victor's fame, like the sound of his battles, dies away. Time will tear many a flower from the garland with which we love to bind the brows of this Age of Progress; but the chivalrous deed, the unselfish devotion, the burning charity, the apostle's zeal will bloom forever. With him who inspired them, with her who fostered them, each holy deed shall shine, when the last wreck of all human progress has vanished—shall live, when time cannot touch one single leaf in the immortal coronal, which virtue's hand has placed upon the brow of the Age of Progress.

## THE DANGER OF THE AGE.

THE history of the Age, considered as an Age of Progress, which I attempted to delineate in my last lecture, may be summed up in a few words. As regards progress in the natural sciences, the nineteenth century stands at the head of ages. Its material progress has revolutionized the industry, commerce, ideas, manners and intercourse of civilized society. It has developed enormous wealth, but, in populous countries, it has produced that fearful disease of modern times, pauperism. With respect to Moral Progress, while crime has assumed novel forms of gigantic iniquity, virtue has risen by its side with a lustre worthy of the bright ages of Christianity.

Thus far, truth and error, virtue and vice, have gained only partial triumphs. Which of them will ultimately obtain the ascendant? Without attempting to decide a question, placed beyond the limit of human foresight, I shall endeavor to-night to point out the peculiar danger of the age—the evil which, unless arrested or checked, must end by ruining our progress.

The predominant evil of the age, its peculiar danger, I take it, is the materialistic spirit. I do not say that materialism is our *only* danger. Pride, sensuality, cupidity spring up forever from human corruption, form the common menace of all time, and explain all the ruins of history. Nor do I refer to that form of materialism which denies the immortality of the soul. Few men in any age will so far abdicate the dignity of manhood, as to choose to rank merely as the first in the scale of the brute creation. The materialism to which I refer, is practical rather than theoretical. It places material interests and materialistic passions above the interests of the soul and the claims of virtue. Materialism, thus defined is the Danger of the Age. I shall briefly consider its extent, its effects, and the means to avert it.

The extent of the danger is easily ascertained by comparing the place which material progress and material interests occupy in popular estimation, with the position assigned to them by reason and religion. Moral progress, religion, virtue should hold the first place in man's esteem: material progress and material interests should occupy a subordinate position. This doctrine does not *condemn* material progress. Let man assert his native dominion over the elements. Let him compel wind and wave and lightning to do his bidding and perform his labor. Let him whiten every sea with the canvas of his fleets, and fill every vale with the hum of his industry. He may embody his ideal of power, strength, beauty, sublimity, in works which imitate, by the grandeur or delicacy of their proportions, the creative thought and the creative act which moulded the flower and built the heavens. Let him "fill the earth and subdue it." All this is but a legitimate assertion of his sovereignty, a proof of his high origin, the gift of God, the fulfilment of the divine benediction. But let him not bend the knee to his own handiwork. By the nobler portions of his being, by the boundless aspirations of his immortal spirit, by the kindling glance of his eye as he gazes up to heaven, the voice of God and the voice of reason tell him, in tones which intelligence cannot mistake, nor corruption deafen, that his first, his chief, his last progress is moral progress; his true course is upward, in the direction of his eternal destiny;—his aspirations, like the mountain cross, the symbol of the soul, should soar to heaven.

Judged by this standard, the age evidently has outstepped the limits within which material interests should be confined. It points to the miracles of its material progress as man's whole progress; to steamboats and steam engines, to net-works of railroads, and telegraph lines, to new systems of commerce and industry, as the great signs of the superiority of its civilization. The materialistic spirit has its temple in the counting-house, where it worships unceasingly at the shrine of the Almighty Dollar. It rules the destinies of nations, dictates war and peace, makes and breaks treaties. It sacrifices a hundred thousand men, sons of the Crusaders, upon the snows of the Crimea, to uphold on the fairest portions of Europe, the sensual standard of Mahometan degradation. The *science* of materialism, is the art of amassing wealth; its code of morals, physical enjoyment. It scorns the disinterested devotion of religious heroes, and the unselfish labor of the cloister; heaps its unmeasured sarcasms on all who choose to despise the earth, and devote their lives to heaven. It creates despotism and cruelty in the higher ranks, dissatisfaction in the lower, restlessness everywhere. You may see its unwholesome workings in the recklessness which makes or squanders a fortune in a day; in rapacity, unchecked by any principle of charity or justice; in craft, cunning and deceit; in the faithless contract, and the gigantic fraud; in the revel which consumes in an hour what would suffice to feed and clothe the poor of a city. You may read it on the faded brow of youth, in the wasted morals of the factory, in the weakening of family ties, in the fierce independence of the stripling. Its history is the long list of wrongs inflicted on the widowed and the fatherless. Its heartlessness would make the poor, like the machines of its industry, mere producers to feed its luxury. Distress, murder, starvation follow in its wake. Its echo is the sigh of the needle-woman, the loud wail of pauperism, the curse of oppressed labor, the muttered sound of socialistic revolutions.

Another sign of the prevalence of the materialistic spirit, is the popular literature of the day. A vast portion of it breathes the very spirit of sensuality. It seeks not its inspiration in the heroic devotion of self-sacrific-

## THE DANGER OF THE AGE. 69

ing virtue, nor yet in the hallowed sphere of disinterested patriotism, nor even in the ennobling associations of a virtuous home. The harp that consecrates its harmonies to a Christian theme, is unheeded, except by a few kindred spirits. To be popular, literature must descend from noble sentiment to corrupt sensation, from the pure regions of virtue, to the contaminated purlieus of vice. Sensual in its ideal, its subject, its tone, its purpose, the expression of covetousness and luxury, it has learned the art of making man's noblest aspirations, his most spiritual sentiments, the panders of sensuality. The materialistic spirit is the reason of the popularity of such authors as Eugene Sue, Alexander Dumas, George Sand. *It is typified in Les Miserables of Victor Hugo.* The multitudinous race of similar writers is one of the saddest signs of the age. Modern society is flooded with their contaminating productions.

I had intended to dwell at some length on the materialistic theories of our world-reformers. A word or two will suffice. Like Voltaire, the mass of them aspire to dethrone God. Like him they denounce Christ, hate his cross, or, while impudently claiming him as their leader,*

---

D. Cortes, B. iii.

aspire to replace the purity of his doctrine by the vileness of their own dogmatism. The fires of the old atheistic revolution have died away on the soil of Europe. Socialistic revolutions have risen from its ashes, and perpetuate its spirit among the wretched multitudes of European Capitals. In our own country, infidel revolutionists boldly parade in the streets with torch and emblazoned banner, in honor of Tom Paine. They denounce death to the Papacy, because the Papacy is the bulwark of Christianity, because the Catholic Church is the sole power on earth that can check the triumph of the materialistic principles, of which they bear the ignominious standard. The Church, indeed, they cannot conquer. She is immortal. Nor is the danger to the martyr who may bleed in the holy cause. While the disciples of materialism shall display their banners in honor of their masters, men of soul will not be wanting to point the finger of scorn at the degraded procession, or sadly say, "There march the great enemies of the human race." While infidelity and vice shall raise a monument to the Apostles of materialism, faith and virtue will come and mourn around the tomb, and inscribe upon its tablets, "Here lie they for whom it were better had they not been born!" But still the spirit of infidelity, the spirit of infidel persecutions, is one of the dark symptoms of the prevalence of materialism. A still darker sign is the assurance which prompts the leaders to put forward in public, the ignominious principles which bear their name. Conscious that the aspirations of the age, far and wide, are kindred to their own, they speak with the unblushing boldness of a criminal in the presence of his worse accomplice.

In what I have said hitherto, I do not mean to imply that materialism has obtained anything like a universal sway. There are myriads in all lands, and in all ranks of society, who have not bowed the knee to Mammon. Till the last breath of materialism is stilled on earth, the Cross of the Redeemer rising aloft over the world, where his own power placed it, as the sign and centre of man's liberation from the thraldrom of matter, will twine the hearts of millions around it in the holy union of pure faith and exalted virtue. Millions will carry high in their own hands the sacred banner of the soul, of which the cross is the immortal symbol.

But though materialism cannot destroy the cross, nor extirpate its followers, it may extirpate civilization and destroy nations. The great danger of materialism to which I wish to direct your attention, is in its destructive effects on civilization and national existence. These effects, whenever the materialistic spirit becomes widely predominant, are not difficult to foretell. No prophet is needed to lift the veil that enshrouds the future. History, with all its voices, proclaims one result of materialism, in all nations in which it ever ruled as the master spirit, and that is, the ruin of civilization first, and, as an inevitable consequence, final, irretrievable national downfall.

> "There is a moral of all human tales,
> 'Tis but the same rehearsal of the past,
> First freedom, and then glory,—when that fails,
> Wealth, vice, corruption,—barbarism at last."

These energetic lines of one of the most gifted of our modern poets, himself at last a sad wreck of sensuality, sum up the entire history of the rise and fall of all civilization, and the story of the rise and ruin of all empires.

Materialism explains the origin and existence of the savage state, the lowest condition of barbarism. Originally, all nations and tribes were civilized, and highly civilized. In the plains of Sennaar before the dispersion of men, all had received the same civilizing traditions transmitted from Adam and Noah to all their descendants. These traditions were variously developed in Chaldæa, Chanaan, Phœnicia, Egypt, and later in Greece and Rome Had history told us how these traditions were obscured or lost in barbarous China, India, Thibet, Japan, or among the savage tribes of Africa, America, and the isles of the Pacific, we should find in every instance, that the great cause of the degradation was the dominion of materialism. It was clearly the cause of the ruin of the splendid civilization which flourished of old in central Asia, and along the coasts of the Mediterranean. The history of materialism is emphatically the history of national degradation and national death.

Nor is it difficult to trace the downward steps by which the degradation is accomplished. What distinguished true civilization from real barbarism, is the dominion of mind over matter. True enlightenment consists in the superiority of mental and moral culture. Like individuals, nations remain really great only so long as the spirit retains its legitimate empire. Barbarism, in its essence, is the dominion of matter over spirit.

Materialism begins by ruining moral greatness, and in ruining it exhausts the very sources of civilization. Intellectual ruin follows. Genius dies in the orgies of sensuality. A corrupt, barbaric taste in art and letters, is succeeded by the arrest of Scientific progress. Civilization is disappearing. A lingering display of barbaric splendor alone survives, portending final destruction, as, on some sultry night-fall gilded masses of lurid storm-clouds foretell the destructive tempest of midnight. The last remnant of material progress is buried amid the ruins of the nation.

Materialism, among us, is far from having reached its last or worst developments. We still possess in our midst so many evidences of true moral greatness, so much of glorious and progressive civilization, that we can hardly realize that the great element of ruin is gnawing at the core of our progress. But let us turn to ancient nations. Materialism embodies the whole philosophy of the history of their downfall. The subject well deserves to be studied at some length.

At an early date in the existence of ancient nations, materialism, in the form of idolatry, had implanted in them the seed of their decadence. In their decline, and when the cause of ruin was developed, we may not discover that species of barbarism which was exhibited in the invasions of the Northern barbarians; but instead of the rough barbarism of the forest, we find the barbarism of an effete civilization, the genteel ruffianism of polished cities, the predominance of craft, deceit, treachery, *cruelty*, all the more malignant because habitually concealed under the smooth forms of polite social intercourse. We find a State civilized upon the surface, barbarous and savage within; a society cold, conceited, harsh, hypocritical, apparently refined, but in reality, cruel, vindictive, cowardly, ignorantly proud or arrogantly vain of a little knowledge; a condition worse in many points, than the barbaric or savage state, combining with the rude vices of the forest, all the exquisite corruption of the effeminate city.

When Rome had reached the zenith of her material power; when Europe, Asia, Africa lay bound in helpless subjection at her feet, it became evident that, in her gradual conquest of the world, she had by degrees concentrated in her bosom all the moral diseases of the earth in their most empoisoned forms. The rival of Greece in art and science, unequalled in wealth and power, she wore in her imperial diadem all of grandeur, power, glory, which earthly genius and earthly success could place upon the brow of the mistress of the world. But not a wreck was left of her moral greatness, no lingering remnant of the comparative purity of her early manners; no trace of the manly genius of her former statesmen; scarce a vestige of the hardy spirit which had rendered her legions invincible on a thousand battle-fields. The burning pages of Tacitus and Juvenal bear witness to her almost incredible vices. Adoring degradation in her gods, she had formed her manners in the image of her debasing worship. She bore upon her brow, in deeply marked lines, which the splendor of her imperial crown could not conceal, the sign of a nation, which, with the fall of its moral greatness has relapsed into barbarism. Effeminacy, treachery, *cruelty*, were stamped there in all the livid hues of infamy. I need only point out her *cruelty*. *Cruelty*,—which in an individual is the seal of savage depravity,—cruelty typified in the savage torturing his captive at the stake,—cruelty, when general in a nation, sets upon it the withering stigma of barbarism. In Rome cruelty was universal. Under Nero the bodies of Christians served as torches to light up her marble squares and the midnight orgies of her princes and people. Her myriads—patrician, knight, high-born lady, and plebeian mob—thronged the steps of the Coliseum to witness the deadly strife of the gladiator. Amid that gorgeous array of Roman pride and power, the Christian martyr alone held aloft the banner of human greatness. He alone, amid a nation of slaves, silent, calm, like his own Great Master, his eyes raised to heaven, his lips smiling with an angel's serenity, while the shouts of fifty thousand persecutors demanded his death;—the Christian Martyr, as his mangled form fell and his blood moistened the arena, told in his silent fortitude that a new era had dawned upon the world. Materialism was conquered, man was free with the freedom of the soul, the immortal freedom of the redeeming cross.

With her moral greatness, Rome had lost the last shadow of her liberties. Slaves to matter, the former rulers of the world, they who had swayed the destinies of Empires, bowed to the vilest ruffian upon whose shoulders the pretorian guard cast away the degraded purple; —bowed in cowering terror to vice incarnate upon the throne, as they bowed to vice divinized upon the altar;— to Tyranny armed with the Furies' scourge to chastise the arrogant degradation that dared to raise its unclean hand to slaughter the saints.

Rome's intellectual greatness, too, was extinguished in the thick darkness of her barbaric licentiousness. Materialism had withered the genius of her poets as materialistic despotism had silenced the voice of her orators. No Virgil rose again to sing the glories of her sires; no Livy to inscribe her varied fortunes upon his "pictured page;" no Horace to inspire her with his martial strain. The only men who towered above their fallen co-temporaries, were those men whom our materialistic age never mentions except with a smile of scorn—the grand old Fathers of the glorious Church of the Catacombs—the Ambroses, the Hilarys, the Augustines, the Chrysostoms, whose lofty genius shed a last ray on the crumbling glories of the persecutor, and announced the "kindling dawn" of a more glorious civilization, silently rising from beneath the shadow of the cross.

The doom of Rome was sealed. Materialism had ruined all preceding empires. It had destroyed her rivals. More than her own arms, the moral degeneracy of other nations had placed in her hands the sceptre of the world. Materialism was destined to be her own ruin. *Ambition* alone cannot destroy a State. A nation which retains its moral energy, may be conquered; it is not therefore ruined; it rises from its fall to greater splendor. But an effeminate, barbaric civilization is powerless. It gives birth to no great leaders; or if, at intervals, an individual rises above the mass of degradation, he finds around him but a cowardly rabble that can no longer be led to victory. Even physical courage, the last survivor of moral degeneracy dies away. Capua makes the soldiers of Hannibal quail upon the field of battle. An effeminate race sinks beneath the tread of the first strong-willed conqueror issuing from his mountain fastnesses, with an army trained to hardships. Babylon succumbs to the yoke of a handful of Persians and Medes. In his degeneracy, the Persian sees his millions hurled back in shame across the Hellespont. Greece, in the decline of her manly virtues, quails before the Macedonian phalanx. The remnant of her national energy revives but a moment under the leadership of Alexander, to die away forever, and leave her to fall with scarce a struggle, under the all-conquering sway of the still manlier Romans. Rome, in her turn, when she lies festering in barbaric corruption amid her golden palaces, falls ingloriously. Her wealth tempts the barbarian hovering on her borders. Her Eagle, ennobled by a thousand years of victory, is trailed in the dust beneath the banner of the woods. Nerveless successors of the Fabii and Scipios, her effeminate legions allow the forest-chieftain to revel in the halls of her Cæsars. The language which had dictated laws to the world, becomes a jargon of barbaric tongues. Where it survives in its purity, in her matchless poets and orators, it lives as an everlasting memorial of her unequaled downfall. Rome might have been regenerated by Christianity, but ere the change was accomplished, vengeance called forth the flood of Northern barbarism upon that land crimsoned with the blood of saints, and writing upon her blood-stained wreck the tragic fate which awaits the persecutor of purity, told the appalling moral of all human degeneracy.

> "History with all its volumes vast,
> Has but one page."

That page is written in its ruins. Ruins are the grand instructors of history. The poet, the philosopher, the historian, the moralist love to linger around the impressive teachers, and learn from their silent eloquence. If you wish to read the destiny which awaits our own civilization, should materialism bring back its ancient corruption, go to the shores of the Mediterranean, the seat of fallen empires; the tale is written on the ivy-clad walls where "Ruin greenly dwells;" in the dreary fragments of a hundred cities, where amid "matted weeds" the pilgrim "stumbles over recollections" of glories dimmed forever in moral degradation. It is written in the still desert, where once the joyful rush of nations thronged to battle; and on the solitary sea-shore, where the wealth of cities gathered the freighted galleys of world-wide commerce. It breathes in the rent arches of the Coliseum, in the silence of the old Martian field, in the triumphal column, where time has preserved, in mockery, the boastful tale of vanished victories. In Rome, ancient civilization has left only its ruins. There and in western Europe, new States have covered the wrecks of the Roman empire with the glories of Christian civilization. In the East the ruins of both Gentile and Christian civilization, mantled in the darkness of Moslem barbarism, and the wreck of Mahometanism, itself silently mouldering in its corruption, present in one view, wherever you turn your footsteps, a three-fold lesson of portentous warning.

"Greece is living Greece no more." "She saw her glories, star by star, expire." Greece! memories from every classic vale and mountain, sad memories of many, many fallen glories, meet and mingle at the mention of thine unrivalled name. O thou who shouldst have been immortal! Alas! that thy worshipped graces planted the fatal tree, under whose softly insidious shade thy genius sank and slumbered, to rise or wake no more! Eleusis, the sensual seat of the mysteries of Cora and Demeter, tells the story of her downfall. The present obscurity of Eleusis* is a fit emblem of her darkened glories. On the hillside of Delphi, not even a fragment of Paphian marble is left, to tell where the sensual son of Athens came to consult his oracular demon. Where Pindar sang and Demosthenes "thundered over Greece," the voice of genius no longer wakes an echo of her former triumphs. On the crags of Pindus the Albanian banditti sing their wild song of plunder. On the shores of Ionia, the lyre of Homer is replaced by the rude ditty of the fierce corsair. And, far more sad, the old Christian chant is silenced by the Muezzin's call from the Minaret. Greece is a land blighted by heaven's malediction. In Christian times, known for heresy and schism and corruption, the land which rejected the pure freedom of the cross, was bruised and crushed under the sensual bondage of the crescent. The Musulman still offers impi-

---

* Now Lepsina.

ous worship in St. Sophia's; his tread defiles Tarsus and Antioch, and Smyrna, and Ephesus, all the hallowed ground consecrated by the early memories of the Apostles. The degenerate descendant of the old Hellenes feebly trims the lamp of liberty on the ruins of the once proud Acropolis. No Areopagus holds its sittings on the deserted hill of Mars; no Amphyctionic council assembles the States of Greece, under the historic mountain shade, at the passes of Thermopylae, to breathe wisdom into her councils. Among the Cyclades, over Idalia and Paphos, still waves the Turkish crescent;—still glances the turbaned host, in light caique, along the bright waters of her own Ægean. Over all the land materialism has traced its saddest memorial of woe; and faith has added there to the moral that other impressive lesson, that the land where sensuality breathes heresy, and schism dares to touch the seamless garment of the Redeemer—is destined sooner or later, to be the land of the despot and the cringing slave.

The "voiceless shores" of Phœnicia, the deserted vales of Judea—they too tell, in their mute eloquence, the same melancholy tale. Tyre, she "whose merchants were princes and her traders the noblest of the earth,"* she who invited all nations to her sensual orgies, is succeeded by the lonely fisherman drying his net upon the silent sea-beach. On the heights of Carmel and Libanus, scarce grows there a solitary representative of the cedars sung by David. Sion is deserted; her streets in mourning; her sons in their immortal wanderings, bear upon their brow the sign of the most appalling of all the fearful triumphs of materialism—the memory of the gloomy deed accomplished by carnalism, eighteen hundred years ago—the memory of the dismal day, darkened by the last sigh of the Creator upon the fearful heights of Golgotha. The hand of the Moslem forbids the Christian to build upon her ruins.

Cast a glance along " Afric's winding shore." It is blasted by the tread of the Mussulman. The coasts of Africa were among Rome's richest provinces. Carthage is but a name. Hippo too is gone. Where was heard the eloquent voice of Cyprian, where Tertullian wrote his burning apologies, and St. Augustine sat at the head of councils, the sun of faith has set in the darkness of sensualism, or casts but a dim twilight

* Isaiah.

glance upon barbarous dwellers. It is a region of Islam barbarism and ruin.

Eastward lies the land of the pyramid and obelisk and labyrinth, the half-forgotten home of ancient learning, the wreck of a civilization as grand as its colossal monuments, as mysterious as its hieroglyphics, and the sources of its rivers. Thither resorted the sages of Greece in the dim old ages of her founders, to learn from the Egyptian priesthood the rudiments of art and law, which made their own nation the noblest of the Gentile world. The civilization of Egypt became degraded like the worship of her ox-god Apis. On her shores, too, rules the Mussulman. The Christian solitary no longer wakes the midnight echoes of Thebais with his sacred hymn. The holy legions long since fled before the tide of Moslem corruption. In the dead stillness of the South Egyptian desert, hundred-gated Thebes spreads her moss-grown columns, shattered remnants of gigantic statues and broken obelisks, over many a mile of barren soil, where once her hundred thousand warriors displayed their shining legions to do battle for the Pharaohs. The jackal's bark, under the ruined portico, replaces the nightly wassail of her million worshippers of Onuphis. Along the rocky tract of Western Egypt, towards the Lybian desert, the Pyramids—huge remnants of forgotten art and gigantic ambition—still rise in their old mountain majesty, mute guardians of ruined edifices, statues, tombs, sphinxes heaped in confusion at their feet. They once overlooked fields fertilized by the sea-like waters of the Nile, or the vast sluices of Lake Moeris, the mightiest reservoir built by human hands :—fields which were the world's granary. Now they look down upon the dreary sands brought by the Simoon from the desert of Sahara. No scion of the ancient race appears on their winding stairway. The very reason of their existence is forgotten. The European traveler vainly asks of the broken sarcophagus in their hollow sides, or the hieroglyphic upon the vaulted granite, to explain the enigma of their destiny—whether meant as tombs for kings or gods. Tombs or temples, it is the same. There they stand, colossal monuments of gigantic downfall. "Forty centuries," said Bonaparte to his legions, "look down upon you from their summits." Vain pride! It is the great voice of eternity which issues from their imperishable depths: the hand of materialism which built them struck the nation down.

Go to the banks of the Euphrates and Tigris. There Nineveh built those famous walls on which three chariots could drive abreast; they have left no trace of their existence. There Babylon, the rival of Nineveh, raised to the heavens, "her tiara of proud towers," the guardians of her hundred brazen gates. They have mouldered to the dust.

The ruin of Assyria, the cradle of the human race, strikingly sums up the whole history of the downfall of nations, and abridges all the sad annals of materialism. All prophecy, from that which foretold the deluge to that which foretells the world's conflagration, repeats, with one voice, that materialism ends in ruin. When corruption has done its worst, if it does not destroy itself, God intervenes for its destruction. He has at his command the floods that engulph the human race, the fires that consume the cities of the plain, the sword of the Persian and the Mede which annihilates Assyrian power.

There is "high festival" in Babylon. It is the ominous eve predicted to all nations who forget their God

*—omni genti obliviscenti Deum.*—No disaster is looked for. No nation which ever fell expected its destruction. Men look for political convulsions, as they look for the storm. The cloud darkens the sky for a moment; it may leave some ruins in its path; but presently the sun breaks through the gloom; the heavens shine with a brighter blue, the field is fresher, the flower sweeter. Like our modern theorizers, men of old looked on present calamity as the harbinger of a more brilliant future, and more splendid progress. Babylon deigns not even to read the prophetic page which contains the "burden of her woe." The festive lamp is lit in all her palaces.

> "And the soft night-breeze through her terrace bowers,
> Bore deepening tones of joy and melody
> O'er an illumined wilderness of flowers;
> And the glad city's voice went up from all her towers."

It is the last outburst of revelry of a splendid but effete and barbaric civilization. All crimes cumulate in this last debauch. The King, the sacrilegious impersonation of the licentiousness of his people, sits enthroned in the gorgeous hall, "high at the stately midnight festival," amid adoring slaves and satraps. Sacrilege flings its last insult up to heaven, and casts in the face of Omnipotence its last impotent defiance. "He who sleeps not," has marked that hour for his own. While the hand of sacrilege raises to its lips the sacred vessels of the Temple, the mysterious shadow moves its fingers along the shining wall. There, full in view, before the cowering throng, is written the enigma of the doom. One of those "who on the willows hung their captive lyres," interprets the fearful vision. The days are numbered, the iniquity is weighed, the sceptre given to the Persian and the Mede.

> "Ere on the brow one fragile rose-leaf fade,
> The sword hath raged through joy's devoted train;
> Ere one bright star be faded from the sky,
> Red flames, like banners, wave from dome and fane;
> Empire is lost and won, Belshazzar with the slain."

Scarce a trace is left of the pride and power of the mightiest of cities that ever rose on earth. The mountain terraces of her hanging gardens have sunk to a level with the soil. The vast palaces of her Kings, which enclosed miles in their gorgeous magnificence, the golden halls where Balthasar "trembled at a shadow," are lost in unsightly pools. No wandering

Arab pitches his tent upon the desolate spot. Each word of prophecy is accomplished. It is the great warning of history—Materialism is the ruin of civilization.

In modern nations, materialism has not yet led to the degradation which was the ruin of all the mighty empires which once rose and flourished and fell in central Asia and on the coasts of the Mediterranean, and ended in bowing nearly all those beautiful regions under the most degraded of anarchic despotism and Mussulman barbarism. We cannot realize the thought that our own civilization will ever sink under the hoof of some new Mahometanism, or fall beneath the anarchic sway of socialistic revolutions. But the principle of ruin, materialism, is the spirit of the age. It is gnawing at the heart of our progress. The corruption it engenders is not self-correcting. The corruption of civilization never was, and never can be self-amending. Left to itself, it grows and spreads and cankers with each rising generation. Sow the seeds of ruin, you must reap the bitter fruit of destruction. The calamities of the age, the socialistic revolutions of Europe, portend ruin, as the storm-cloud portends the tempest.

Should society reach the maturity of its materialistic tendency, the ruins of our civilization, proportioned to the light of Christianity from which it fell, to the broad continents it covers, to the mighty powers accumulated by long centuries of progress. would present a wreck more piteous than all the ruins of all empires. The ruins of Babylon, Nineveh, Egypt, Greece, Rome, all combined would lose their terrors in the unexampled horrors of the new disaster.

But there is a remedy for the evil. There is a power that can stem the tide of materialistic corruption. The remedy is the triumph of the spirit over matter. The power is the Church. "He plucks up the foundation of all society," said Plato, two thousand years ago, "who plucks up religion."* Materialism destroys religion. Gentile religion, itself materialistic, served but to hasten the ruin of society. The Christian religion, the Church alone, possesses the spiritualizing power necessary to preserve society from the destructive dominion of the materialistic spirit; while materialism, by destroying religion, produces barbarism and ruin. The Church, by rendering the spirit predominant over

* Laws B. x.

matter, is the author of civilization and progress, and the condition of their duration.

In this very hall on the ceiling above your heads, Christian art, in a happy hour of inspiration, has delineated the true story of the triumph of the spirit over matter. Yonder, in that halo of pure light with his modest train of virgin virtues around him, marching to the conquest of the laughing deities, whose smile was the destruction of ancient civilization, the genius of Christianity, bearing in his hand the symbol of the crucified, still holds out the promise that redeems the world from the dominion of the principle of ruin,—the cross—the immortal symbol, the immortal triumph of the spirit.

Embodied in her who saved society, thirteen hundred years ago, from the mingling tide of Barbaric and Roman degradation; impersonated in her who conquered Rome by the blood of her martyrs, and the Northern woodman by her holy purity and holy zeal; living in her who was sent from Olivet, with the last blessing of the Redeemer upon her, (to *teach* the nations,) the genius of Christianity goes forth among the nations, and with the fire of faith enkindles the undying light of Christian civilization,—plants the cross above all its works, breathes the spirit, the living, the immortal spirit of the cross into the very souls of nations. It is the genius of order, the genius of liberty, the genius of progress; the eternal foe to the materialistic spirit, the anarch, the despot, the myriad-handed destroyer of nations. That genius is the Church,—the grand Church of the Catacombs, the glorious old Church of the Middle Ages, the great civilizer —the Church of all time, the true Church of God.

A glance at her past action is sufficient to prove her present power; for born of God, like God, she is unchangeable. In all time, her triumph is the triumph of the soul; her power, the hope of progressive and permanent civilization.

Thirteen hundred years ago, the North poured upon Central and Southern Europe its horded stores of barbarism. From savage Sarmatia, the Vandal and Alan and Sueve, came like an Eastern whirlwind, under the savage leadership of Genseric. Alaric brought his ruthless Gothic hordes from the borders of the Baltic. From the bleak regions of Scythia, Attila, a name of terror, appeared at the head of his relentless Huns. Germany and Scandinavia sent forth the wild Burgundian and Visigoth, the Norman and the Lombard. The fields of France and the vineyards of Spain were a waste; the cities of Italy in ashes. On the Alps and Appenines and Pyrenees the rude banner of the woods replaced the Roman Eagle. The spirit of the barbarian was typified in this one word of Attila, "I am the scourge of God,—the hammer of the earth; where my horse treads, grass never grows." The spirit of the barbarian was fierce cruelty, the absolute dominion of materialism over the savage nation of the forest.

From out the mingled mass of vice, ignorance, thirst of blood and plunder, the spiritualizing genius of the Church formed the glorious civilization, and all the boasted progress of Modern nations. She breathed upon the chaos, and a new world sprang forth from its bosom. The barbarian had brought the sword that murders for the joy of slaughter, the torch that burns for the glory of the conflagration. Hatred of arts—the anarchy of the forest —was all his dower. The Church came to him with the olive branch of peace, wreathed around his brow the laurel of art and science, breathed into his soul, with the spirit of her faith, the glorious spirit of Christian civilization.

Free herself, born of God's own freedom, the Church made the barbarian free—free with her own godlike freedom. To her,—to her alone,—belongs all the high honor of our boasted liberties. For the first time in the history of idolatrous Europe, she placed liberty upon its true basis. She said "obey God, and obey man only for God's sake; all other obedience degenerates into slavery." The spirit which made Thermopylæ immortal, and consecrated the soil of Marathon and Platæa, fades before the freedom which she gave, the God-like freedom won on Golgotha, and sealed in the Flavian amphitheatre, and on all the fields of Rome, with the blood of twelve millions of her own free martyrs. Greeks and Romans, in their best days, were slaves, trebly slaves, bound heart and hand, to their gods, to their States, to their own hearts; fettered with a threefold chain, not the less inglorious because the bondman hugged the gilded fetters as the emblem of his glory. Upon the brow of the barbarian the Church placed the triple halo of civil, moral, and religious liberty. Religious liberty: She made the sons of the forest martyrs like those who fell in the Coliseum, and wrote with their own blood their charter of immortal religious freedom. Moral freedom: She sent forth the sons of the barbarian as new Apostles, to plant on every mountain-top the glorious sign of man's moral regeneration. Civil freedom: in her hands the nations felt that the liberties she had given them were safe. Despots quailed before her. Her spirit nerved the arm of the Christian Visigoth in his eight hundred years of struggle against the Moor. The spirit of her freedom arrested the crescent in its despotic march.

When that new barbarism, Mahometanism, issued from the desert of Arabia, with torch and scimitar, to mantle Europe in the ten-fold darkness of its sensualism, she called on the converted son of the Hun and Vandal, of the Frank and Norman, to gird on the sword, hold back the despot, and save the new civilization her own genius had created. The new war-cry, the Crusaders' shout of battle, "God wills it," "God wills it," spreading from Clermont, borne along the castled crags of the Rhine, caught up by every echo in the Alps and Pyrenees and Appenines, reverberating along the shores of the Mediterranean and Atlantic, thundering along the waters of the Baltic and the North sea, led forth the sons of the barbarian to the grandest battles ever fought for human freedom.

Degenerate sons of glorious sires, unworthy inheritors of the brilliant civilization bequeathed by the sons of the cross, the men of our day turn, in their grovelling baseness, upon their champions, and tell us in every form of print and speech, tell us, in the name of their own degraded materialistic spirit, that the Crusades,—O shame of shames!—were the very madness of religious fanaticism. Madness, fanaticism, indeed! It was the madness which redeemed us from Moslem Slavery. It was the fanaticism, which, raising over all Europe, the glorious battle shout of "God wills it," "God wills it," and placing the invincible cross upon the mailed armor of our forefathers, hurled back the sensual march of Moslem degradation. Fanaticism indeed! Why was civilized Europe saved? Because Rome was there—because the grand old faith of Rome still held undivided sway over the nations, which have since presumed to spurn the mother, who gave them the very life of all their boasted institutions. Wherever Rome had been rejected in the days of the Crusades, the crescent, to this hour, usurps the place of the redeeming cross. From the borders of the Danube to the banks of the Indus—on the classic banks of the Achelous, on the wrecks of Egypt and Assyria and Ionia, over all the lands of ancient culture, the Kiosk and Minaret still stand amid ruins, as emblems of effeminacy and barbarism. If we are civilized to-day, if we are free, it is owing to the cross upon the brazen armour of our sires, to the bannered cross, to the sacred battle-shout of the Crusader, to the Christian "God wills it," which reverberated in answer to the Moslem shout of " Allah Acbar," from the walls of Salem to the walls of Vienna, from the waters of the Nile to the waters of Lepanto.

Then, too, among the sons of the barbarous Northern forest, rose that other lofty spirit, Christian Chivalry, not the maudlin counterfeit chivalry of the modern romance, not the skulking mimicry gathered in cowardly midnight council, but the very condemnation of all the low conceptions of materialism, the generous pure spirit of those famous Knights, who, under their steel corselets, bore the soul of high honor, refined courtesy, manly munificence, which have given its exalted meaning to the name of Christian chivalry. Then faith bowed with the reverence of religion to human dignity, degraded by Gentilism; then the prowess of the brave was the shield of the weak; mercy softened the native roughness of battle; truth sincerely pledged her Knightly word, whose breach, in those hearts nurtured in Christian loyalty, was a disgrace from which no valor on tented field or castled steep would redeem the culprit. Created by the spiritualizing genius of the Church, formed by her own hands out of the relentless natures which the forest had poured upon her, growing under her inspiration, the spirit of glorious old Catholic chivalry forms the very ideal of exalted manhood.

That ideal, like all her ideals of greatness, the Church embodied in an institution which copied her own perpetuity. On the borders of European civilization, to guard its approaches against the ruffian Moslem, she placed a guard, in the dress of a religious warrior the noblest of the sons of the Norman, Frank and Visigoth, the Knight of St. John, the grand impersonation of unconquerable chivalry. Faithful to his deputed trust for five centuries, the religious Knight stood sentinel under the walls of Jerusalem, on the shores of Rhodes, in the rocky fortress of Lavalette, of Malta. In peace, the generous hospitaler, the open handed friend of the pilgrim and the stranger, the tender nurse of the sick; in war, the noble Knight of Malta stood a living bulwark against which broke, wave on wave, each furious shock of the Janizary until the last of the glorious crusaders, Pope St. Pius V., Don Juan of Austria, and their valiant fleet of generous soldiers of the cross, shattered forever the Moslem power on the memorable waters of Lepanto.

Ere the age of the Crusaders was passed, the Church had taught the Lombard, and Norman, and Frank, and Saxon, and Goth—those who had come with torch and axe in hand, levelling monument and temple, school and library in indiscriminate destruction—to build the lofty Gothic arch, to stain its windows with pictured crimson, green, and gold, to adorn its niches and pinnacles with statuary of Grecian mould and Christian purity; to embody the ideal of Christian sublimity in the massive marble walls of such Cathèdrals as that of Milan, soaring with its crown of four thousand statues of breathing marble, a glorious symbol of her conquest over the rude barbarian of the Gothic forest; to transform Grecian art in the Cathedral of St. Peter's, lifting its stupendous dome upon its huge columns five hundred feet above the lingering remnants of ancient Roman grandeur, and carrying, in the "harmonious vastness" of its proportions, the embodied triumph of her conquest over the materialism of pagan gods. She taught them to open the learned halls of the universities of Paris, Oxford, Cambridge, Prague, Salamanca; and gather within their precincts from ten to thirty thousand scholars, a living garland woven by her own hands, as another token of the fulness of her triumph. She made the sons of the barbarian, theologians and philosophers like Albertus Magnus and St. Thomas Aquinas, mighty names whose equals our progressive age has not produced, whose peers the world may never behold again, unless they spring from the fertilizing genius of the Catholic Church. She taught them to attune the lyre of Homer to Christian themes, to awaken more than the burning eloquence of Cicero and Demosthenes in the cause of human liberty and sanctity. Her spirit led Columbus across the deep, to open new worlds to the civilization of the cross. It created the press, the boasted powers of the press, the weapon which the materialistic spirit of the age incessantly wields to assail her, and which her own hand blessed and still blesses as the great instrument of human progress. Her spirit is the hope of modern civilization. Whatever her enemies may say, the great glory of the *past* is hers. The nations she civilized may have learned to scorn her; her own children may revive the spirit of pagan persecution;—despising the grand old Church, whose labors conquered and softened and humanized the soul of the barbarian, the age may call the period of her conquest the Dark Ages. Deeming, or affecting to believe, her spirit hostile to light and liberty and progress, and to unite all that is despotic and debased in the past, and the present, and the future, it may name her Babylon, Apollyon, and Antichrist. But her history is written on all the monuments of modern civilzation. Truth raises her voice from field, and vale, and mountain, and city, cultivated, civilized, adorned by her eighteen hundred years of thankless labor. To her, to her alone, we owe the unnumbered Christian glories by which our civilization overshadows all the splendors of Gentile culture; to her, the ten thousand asylums with which she has crowned the globe as with a diadem of charity; to her, the strong heart that redeems the captive with its own liberty; the angel's wing that shields the couch of the orphan boy; the voice that gladdens the dark approaches of the great destroyer; the light that illumes the portals of eternity; the virtues which bloom for heaven. Her march through time, like the footsteps of her founder, is marked by the blessings she has showered upon the nations.

The Church to-day may rise in her old majesty, and in the person of Pius IX., the glorious successor of her long line of Pontiffs, wave her hand over all the glories of your progress and boldly say, "These are the fruits of MY devotion." These are the deeds done by the sons of those children of the forest, redeemed and civilized and led by my own hand to the era of glorious progress. The spirit which has made them great is but the breath of my own spirit; their light but a spark of the torch which my hand enkindled in the darkness of their sires.

The Church is the hope of the *future*. Should Materialism triumph, in some future generation; should infidelity, barbarism, socialistic anarchy, ever rise on the ruins of the civilization she created; should modern societies fall as fell the ancient,—the Church alone, amid the wreck, would uphold the banner honored by two thousand years of progress. Amid the ruins of freedom, she would protest for liberty, and sternly, as of old, in the face of the tyrant, refuse to bow the knee to Belial or Moloch. She might bleed, but surrender

—never, never! Should faith expire amid the orgies of sensualism, the Church, mourning over the descendants of her early martyrs, over the fallen children of those who hallowed her early history by their virgin purity, lingering, while hope remained, around the ruins of cities which grew to might and brilliancy under her gaze, sorrowing over the wreck of nations which she had nurtured to greatness—praying still, like Him who sent her, for each ungrateful soil that rejects her, —mourning, she would turn her steps to other lands less unworthy of her blessings. The sun of faith, accompanying her footsteps, leaving the old lands of civilization to moulder in the thickening darkness of barbarism, would rise in the freshness of a new morn on the isles of the Pacific; or returning to the lands which saluted its earliest dawn, shine once more in the fulness of its midday splendor on those desolate Asiatic shores, where the Apostle's voice first spoke peace and brought civilization to the degenerate Gentile. From her new home, from the new civilization created by her spirit the Church would send back new Apostles to the darkened lands that scorned her, and bid them bring, with the fires of faith, the lost light of art and science, replant the fallen tree of freedom, and water it at need with their hearts' best blood. The Church is the only hope of the present. Alone blest and consecrated on the heights of Olivet to vivify all that is grand and ennobling in the human soul, to communicate her own purity to all that is winning or sublime in art or science, blessing with heaven's blessing, from her own full heart, all the marvels of material progress, the Church, the ever living genius of Christianity, will check, and, let us hope, conquer the Danger of the Age.

The last hope of our civilization is in the immortal mission she has received from on high. Sprung from God's own being, the connecting link between earth and heaven, the sole inheritor of undying promises, she asserts with more than human authority, the great law which lies at the root of all true civilization—the supremacy of mind over matter. Gifted with powers equal to her mission, while she illumines the mind, she imparts to the will the generosity which can despise the earth; the heroism which renders nations invincible; the virtues which form the true glory of all human civilization. Immortal with the immortality of Him, whose being is the soul of her own existence, she communicates her immortality to the nations which listen to her voice, and makes them share in the divinity of her own existence. All else decays. Cities crumble, the ruins of dynasties and empires are heaped around her in her march through time. The mighty rush of error dies at her feet, the power of the persecutor is bowed before her. When the tyrant is gone to the dust, and the loud voices which predicted her downfall are hushed and forgotten, she lives to teach and redeem the nations;—she lives, and will live, leaning on Almighty power. She will go through the nations and the ages till eternity shall strike the passing knell of all human things. Because she is thus invincible, because she is thus alone the most perfect of all earthly images of God's immensity, eternity, and power, while her voice remains to condemn error, and her power to redeem men from the thraldrom of matter, nations may rise again to the glory from which they fell. Whatever our age may deem, should modern society survive the ruin which threatens it, other times will look back to her labors in the ages which are opening, as we look back to her works in the past, and attribute the brightest splendor of their civilization to her devotion. May that hour of triumph come! May the materialistic spirit thus be conquered! May the influence which is gathering around her the purest and noblest of the earth, be widened till the nations which have left her, return to her bosom! May the myriads of pure hearts that crowd around her altars, swell till their numbers expand into countless millions! May the light of unselfish zeal and heroic devotion, enkindled by her, still shining bright and spotless through the thickening darkness of materialism, spread till the world is enkindled by its flames. The hour of HER triumph is the hour when shall cease the Danger of the Age.

www.ingramcontent.com/pod-product-compliance
Lightning Source LLC
Chambersburg PA
CBHW020153170426
**43199CB00010B/1011**